PANINI BOOKS

Art Attack Annual 2007 is published under license by Panini Publishing, a division of Panini UK Limited. Office of publication: Panini House, Coach & Horses Passage, The Pantiles, Tunbridge Wells, Kent TN2 5UJ. This publication may not be sold, except by authorised dealers, and is sold subject to the condition that it shall not be sold or distributed with any part of its cover or markings removed, nor in a mutilated condition. Printed in Italy. ISBN: 1-904419-98-4

£6.99

D1139373

LET'S HAVE AN ART ATTACK!

WELCOME TO THE ART ATTACK ANNUAL 2007!

Turn the pages and you'll find loads of fun things to make and do. From papier maché to colouring, painting tips to drawing techniques, this book has everything you need to take the plunge and get creative! And remember, you don't have to be a great artist to Art Attack!

Neil Buchanan

WHAT'S INSIDE!

HINTS & TIPS!

PAPIER MACHÉ MODELS

Most 3D projects are covered with several layers of papier maché. This is really easy to make - all you need is newspaper, PVA glue and water.

Mix one part PVA glue with two parts water. Tear up strips of newspaper and use the glue mixture to paste them onto your model.

You could use kitchen paper or toilet roll instead of newspaper.

Cover your model with at least two or three layers of papier maché and leave it to dry overnight.

After you've painted your model, brush on a layer of PVA glue. It will look white at first but goes clear when it's dry, giving you a fabulous, shiny finish!

ALWAYS USE SAFETY SCISSORS!

PAINTING TECHNIQUES

Watercolours are useful as you can dilute them with water to make them transparent, or build up layers to make a more solid colour.

Try painting on damp paper. Dab on tiny spots of colour and watch the paint as it spreads out. Use a brush to paint stripes of colour which will run into each other.

Poster paints or acrylics are good for painting your finished paper maché models as they give a good covering.

MIXING COLOURS

If you don't have many paints, you can mix them together to get more colours. Try the following combinations:

RED + YELLOW = ORANGE
YELLOW + BLUE = GREEN
RED + BLUE = PURPLE

Add white or black to make lighter or darker shades.

USEFUL STUFF

Old newspapers
Cardboard box card
Empty cereal boxes
PVA glue
Empty cardboard tubes (from toilet rolls, clingfilm etc)
PVA glue
Balloons
Safety scissors
Kitchen paper
Sticky tape
Colouring pens
Paints & paintbrushes
Pencils

DRAWING TECHNIQUES

If you're not that confident, start by draw a picture lightly in pencil then go over it in pen. You can rub out the lines once the ink is dry and no-one will ever know!

Practise different techniques like shading, stippling and cross-hatching. This is where you add detail to a picture with shadows, dots and overlapping lines, as shown below.

REMEMBER TO ASK AN ADULT BEFORE USING THINGS FROM THE KITCHEN!

ART ATTACK

Cut three pieces of thick card approximately 70cm x 15cm. Cut five smaller squares measuring 15cm x 15cm. Tape them together as shown, making sure the shelves are fixed firmly in position as they will need to take the weight of your CDs.

Stand the shelves onto another piece of thick card and draw a base shape slightly larger than the bottom of the shelves, with rounded corners. Cut this out and tape the shelves to it as shown.

Cut three pieces of thin card long enough to fit from the top of your shelves to the base. (The exact measurements will depend on the size of your base.) Tape these in place and stuff the gaps with scrunched-up newspaper.

Cover the whole thing with three layers of papier maché and leave it to dry.

5

To make the head, roll a piece of thin card into a slight cone shape and tape it in place. Stuff with scrunched-up newspaper, making a rounded end for the nose and the back of the head.

6

Cut two cardboard ears and make two rolls of card for the horns. Stuff these with small balls of newspaper and tape another two small balls of newspaper to the tops. Tape the horns and the ears to the top of the head.

7

Once the shelves are dry, tape the head into position. Cover the whole thing in two layers of papier maché and leave it to dry.

8

Paint your giraffe as shown, then when it's dry you can fill it with CDs!

BIRO 'N' WASH

HERE'S A WAY TO CREATE A MOODY AND ATMOSPHERIC PICTURE USING A SIMPLE PEN AND WASH TECHNIQUE.

YOU WILL NEED:

Black ballpoint pen, very watery black paint, or watered-down black ink, paper

TRY IT YOURSELF!

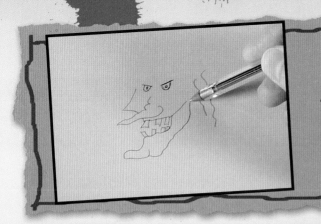

1 Ballpoint pens are very versatile and they're great for sketching. Just draw with the pen as though it's a pencil. Start with a few lines. Just like a pencil, you can press harder for darker lines, or lighter for wispy lines. You can use coloured paper if you like. Here I'm using light grey.

2 If you want, you can sketch in pencil first and rub out the lines later. The great thing about ballpoint pens is that if you go over the lines to alter them, it gives the picture a really sketchy, scratchy feel that's quite spooky.

3 When it comes to shading the picture, use the hatching technique. Just draw lots of lines going in the same direction. You don't need to be neat! You can make darker areas even darker by hatching more lines across the ones you've already done, but in the other direction.

4 Now for the wash! I'm using very watered-down black ink, although you can use watered-down watercolour paint if you like – but it must be very watery!

5 Just brush it on very lightly. You can even use a bit more ink or paint to create a darker shade, too. The great thing about this technique is that the ballpoint pen lines don't run when you wash over them.

HOW TO DRAW...

12

THINGS THAT GO

CUTE COTTAGE

Start with a round base - the circle of polystyrene from a pizza box is ideal. Then make the walls of the house from cardboard, taping them in place near the edge.

2 For a roof, use a plastic or cardboard fruit punnet. Cut it in half, then slot the two halves together so they overlap and tape it in place. Trim off the edge of the base behind the house.

3 Mix kitchen roll with PVA glue to make a pulp. Use lumps of this to create a wall and some shrubs around the base. Stick on a chimney made from a cut-down toilet roll tube.

4 To make the tree bind a stick with paper. Use a pipe cleaner for branches. Use another stick to make a washing line pole. Glue these in place on the base.

PVA

5 Cover everything with three layers of papier maché. Leave it to dry.

6 Finally, paint your model. Create a stone effect on the house, path and walls. Paint green grass and shrubs and add a washing line. Stick on some dried foliage, flowers or leaves to finish the tree.

15

ARTY ACTIVITIES

SPOT THE DIFFERENCE!

See how long it takes you to spot five differences between these two pictures of Neil!

Answers: Eye colour, paint colour, logo on top, paintbrush missing, paintbrush added.

FIND THE COLOURS!

Can you find the ten colours in the grid below?

RED
ORANGE
YELLOW
GREEN
BLUE
PURPLE
PINK
BROWN
BLACK
WHITE

s	d	o	t	y	h	i	r	e	f
o	r	a	n	g	e	u	j	g	e
u	e	h	e	t	h	h	l	b	t
p	d	d	c	y	g	e	l	i	i
l	t	f	u	s	p	r	u	o	h
s	b	p	u	r	p	l	e	c	w
g	l	i	g	u	t	m	k	e	h
h	a	n	j	p	b	r	o	w	n
e	c	k	n	b	x	i	d	f	i
f	k	p	w	c	f	l	y	s	t

16

MIX 'N' MATCH!

Which two paint tubes are an exact match?

Ⓐ Ⓑ Ⓒ Ⓓ Ⓔ Ⓕ

Answers: A and D.

GET COUNTING!

How many pencils and paintbrushes can you see in the pile below?

FAKE CAKE!

CAN'T BAKE? JUST FAKE! MAKE THIS ART ATTACK BIRTHDAY CAKE FOR SOMEONE SPECIAL!

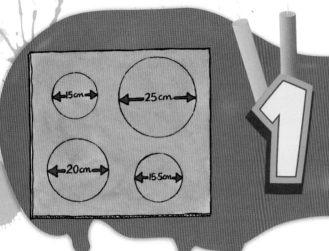

1 Cut four circles, one 25cm in diameter, one 20cm, one 15.5cm and one 15cm. You could use compasses to draw the circles, or different sized plates.

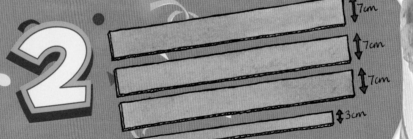

2 Cut three strips of corrugated card, 7cm wide to form the sides of the cake. (Leave them long and trim to fit later.) Cut a strip 3cm wide for the lid.

3 Cut a 30cm square base. Make the bottom cake tier by attaching a strip of card to the largest circle by taping it to the edges. Stick this to the base.

YOU WILL NEED:

Pencil, ruler, cardboard, different sized plates, pair of compasses, bendy card, sticky tape, newspaper, kitchen roll, PVA glue, paints, ribbon.

4

Tape another cardboard strip to the medium-sized circle and fix this to the top of the bottom cake tier with sticky tape. Tape another strip to the 15cm circle and stick this to the top, circle-side down.

5

Tape the 3cm strip to the 15.5cm circle to make the lid. Make sure the lid fits loosely on top of the cake.

6 Cover the whole cake with three layers of papier maché, paying attention to all the joins and keeping it neat. Leave it to dry.

7 Dilute one part PVA glue with four parts water and add some torn-up kitchen paper. Leave it to soak until you have a gooey pulp. Take small peanut sized lumps, mould them with your fingertips and stick around the edges of each cake tier to form icing.

8 To make candles, cut a drinking straw into three equal pieces and push a length of string through the centre of each one. Wrap each straw with a strip of torn-up paper brushed with diluted PVA glue. Stick the candles to the lid using the pulp.

9 Paint the cake white all over and let it dry. (You may need a couple of coats.) Paint the icing and candles. Write a message on top of the cake with paint. Leave it to dry.

FINALLY TIE SOME RIBBON ROUND EACH CAKE TIER. YOU CAN FILL THE TOP CAKE WITH SWEETS BEFORE GIVING TO SOMEONE AS A BIRTHDAY TREAT!

STAY IN LINE!

Place the tip of your pen or pencil on a blank sheet of paper and take it for a walk. You can do this with your eyes shut, if you like!

Start at one side and work towards the other without taking the pen off the page.

You can draw an actual picture like these examples...

....or how about covering the paper with a network of overlapping lines? You could colour the resulting shapes or fill them with patterns.

TRY IT YOURSELF...
TAKE A LINE FOR A WALK!

THE BIG ART ATTACK!

CHECK OUT THIS DAREDEVIL STUNT BIKE JUMPING THROUGH A FLAMING HOOP ... OR IS IT?!

SKY HIGH!

CLOUD COVER!

Create a blue background with acrylic paints. Mix white and blue paint to make pale blue.

Crumple up a sheet of kitchen paper, dip it into white acrylic paint and dab it on to the background to create fluffy clouds.

NIGHT SKY!

Blend two shades of blue - dark blue and a more turquoise shade - to make the background.

Dip a jam jar lid into pale yellow paint and press on to the background. Fill the shape in with more paint. Use the wrong end of your paintbrush to add tiny white stars.

SNOW FALL!

Mix a mid blue colour and paint it all over the background.

For small flakes, dip the end of a pencil into white paint and dab to make dots. For larger flakes, use a thin paintbrush to flick the paint outwards to form a star shape.

SUNSET STRIP!

Paint the background dark blue then paint a strip of orange along the bottom, blending the edges together.

Mix up a paler shade of orange, dip crumpled-up kitchen paper into the paint and dab it onto the background to make clouds that look like they're lit up by the setting sun.

OCTOPUT!

CREATE THIS OCTOPUS FOR YOUR WALL TO PUT YOUR THINGS ON!

YOU WILL NEED:
Cardboard box card, pen, safety scissors, string, newspaper, egg boxes, paint.

YOU CAN PUT ANYTHING ON IT - LIKE JEWELLERY, PHOTOS OR NOTES TO YOURSELF. THE EGG BOX SLITS ARE HANDY FOR PUSHING THINGS IN, LIKE THIS HANKY.

YOU CAN MAKE AN OCTOPUT IN ANY SIZE AND DECORATE IT HOWEVER YOU LIKE!

TRY IT YOURSELF!

25

First, draw an octopus with only four legs dangling down. The head is a sort of ball shape, and the legs are S-shaped with a spiral at the end. The legs need to be about 4cm wide at the top. Cut out the whole shape.

Now the other four legs. Place the shape onto another piece of cardboard box card and draw around the top of the head. Then draw another four legs - popping up above the others. Move the first shape away, and join up the legs like this.

Now cut out the shape. Use a pencil to carefully pierce two holes through the head. You could put some sticky tack behind to protect the surface you're working on!

Thread some string through the holes and tie it together to make a loop going through. This will be used to hang up the octoput when it's finished.

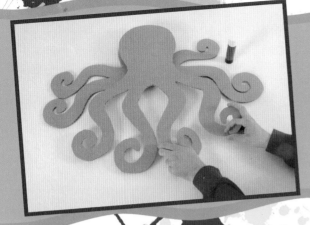

Line up the two head shapes, making sure the string loop is sticking out of the back, and glue them together to create an eight-legged octopus!

Draw on an octopus face and some suckers running down the legs and on the head. Make some newspaper rings like these and cut the bumpy bits from egg boxes, making slits in the tops to create larger rings. Tape them down the legs of the octopus to make 3D suckers.

Using PVA glue mixed in equal parts with water, cover the whole thing with two layers of kitchen roll. Be careful not to go over the slits in the egg box bits!

Put another layer of PVA glue and water mixture over the top, and leave it to dry. Now you can paint your octoput however you like! The suckers will appear to stick out more if you paint them a lighter colour.

27

CRYPT-IC CAT!

HOW ABOUT AN ANCIENT EGYPTIAN CAT DOORSTOP OR PAPER WEIGHT?

YOU WILL NEED
Large or small plastic bottle, sand or stones, newspaper, sticky tape, card, PVA glue, paint, black marker pen, beads.

1 Half-fill a plastic bottle with sand or stones, then replace the lid tightly. Wrap a piece of card around the lid and stick it down.

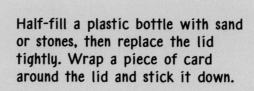

2 Crumple a sheet of newspaper into a tight ball, bind it with sticky tape and glue it on top of the bottle. Cut a pair of ears from cardboard and glue them onto the head.

3 Cover your model with four layers of papier mâché and leave it to dry until it's rock hard.

4 Paint the cat white and let it dry. Draw patterns all over it using pencil. You can look up ancient Egyptian patterns in school books or at the library.

5 Paint the patterns using earthy colours. Use gold paint for the finer details. Paint hieroglyphics (ancient Egyptian picture writing) on the sides.

6 Finally, when the paint is dry, tie some beads around the cat's neck.

29

HOW TO DRAW...

IF YOU'RE WILD ABOUT ANIMALS, YOU'LL LOVE THESE CARTOON CREATURES!

WILD ANIMALS

SPACED OUT!

1 Blow up two large balloons to the same size. Cover the rounded ends in three layers of papier maché and leave them to dry.

2 Pop the balloons and remove them. Make a hole in the top of one papier mache shell and thread a strong piece of string through it. Thread a rectangle of card onto the end, for extra strength, then tie a knot to secure it in place.

3 Join the two halves together with tape, then cover the whole thing in two layers of papier maché and leave it to dry.

4 Make the planets, stars, rocket and satellite as shown over the page.

5 Cut a hoop from thick card, big enough to go around the large planet with space in between.

SET UP YOUR OWN SOLAR SYSTEM WITH THIS COOL SPACE MOBILE!

YOU WILL NEED

Balloons, newspaper, PVA glue, string, cardboard, sticky tape, cocktail sticks, paints, paintbrush, egg box.

Hold it in place and ask an adult to help you tape four cocktail sticks to the hoop, then make holes in the planet as shown. Push the cocktail sticks into the holes and tape them in place. This will help your mobile balance. Cover the tape with papier maché and leave it to dry.

6

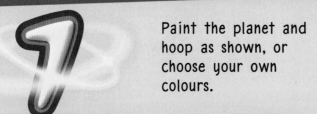

7 Paint the planet and hoop as shown, or choose your own colours.

8 Make holes in the hoop and thread the pieces of string attached to the smaller items through, fastening with a knot. Now you're ready to hang up your mobile!

PLANETS

To make the planets, scrunch up balls of newspaper and hold them in shape with sticky tape. Tape on a piece of string, then cover with a layer of papier maché.

SATELLITE

For the satellite, cut a rectangle of card and carefully score lines along it as shown (ask an adult to help). Fold along the lines to make a hexagon, then fasten it with tape. Attach a piece of string as before, then cover the satellite with papier maché including the ends.

SPACE SHUTTLE

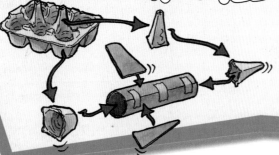

To make a space shuttle, roll up a piece of thin card to make a tube. Cut the pointy part from the inside of an egg box to make the nose and tape it in place. Use one of the cone shapes to make the tail. Cut out two wings and a fin from cardboard and tape them in place. Tape on a piece of string, cover the model with papier maché, then paint it once it's dry.

STARS

Cut some star shapes from cardboard, glue or tape on a piece of string and paint them yellow.

Castle of Fright!

Create some ghostly goings-on in the castle of fright and give yourself a shiver this Hallowe'en!

YOU WILL NEED:
Thin card, safety scissors, glue, felt tip pens or coloured pencils, white fabric, black felt tip pen.

WHAT TO DO:

1 Draw a simple castle on thin card. Make sure it has round windows.

2 Colour in the picture and then cut out the windows.

3 Cut out squares from white fabric. Poke them through the windows and stick them in place at the back. Draw ghostly faces on them.

4 Finally, stick the picture onto card and trim it to fit.

35

SNACK ATTACK!

This loopy lunch box looks great and is fun to make!

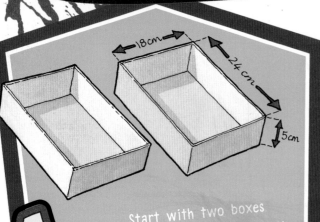

1 Start with two boxes measuring about 24cm x 18cm x 5cm. Find a pair of cardboard boxes the right size or assemble them yourself from cardboard box card.

2 Stick them together using strong tape to form a hinge. Cut 4cm wide strips of card to fit the length and width of one of the boxes. Stick these inside, half in and half out, to form a lip around the edge.

3 Cover the box with three layers of papier maché, avoiding the hinge. Leave it open while it dries.

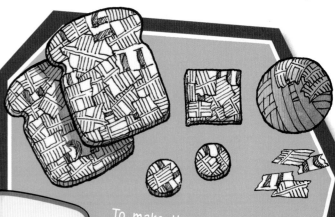

4 To make the orange, crumple newspaper into a tight ball and bind it with sticky tape. For the sandwich, cut bread, cheese and tomato shapes from card. Cover everything with three layers of papier maché.

NEW

CRUNCH

SALT and

lunch

5

To make a packet
of crisps, start with a
rectangle of card. Tape
folded, crumpled paper
to either side and then
cover with three layers
of papier maché and
leave it to dry.

6

lunch

CRUNCH

Paint the lunchbox and
design a lid. Finally, paint
the sandwich, orange and
packet of crisps.

MOONLIGHTING

FIND OUT HOW TO DRAW THINGS IN THE MOONLIGHT!

YOU WILL NEED:

Chalk, black paper.

1 First, draw a moon using white chalk. Use your finger to smudge it a little, then add in some chalk semicircles around it for clouds. Smudge them too. Next, draw a few lines onto the clouds to give them definition.

4 If you draw a city scene, don't forget that at night there would still be some lights on! Use a piece of yellow chalk to give the lights a tinge of colour.

2 Then draw the outlines of whatever is in your picture, using the smudged moon as a guide to what the light will be shining on. I've drawn a night-time city scene.

3 Try to draw the objects in your picture lightly and don't smudge them as much as the moon. Things that have their own light – like a street lamp – need smudging in the direction their light shines.

5 To make the car headlights, draw some white circles of chalk and add a tiny dot of red underneath each one to look like indicators. To finish, smudge the two colours together.

TRY IT YOURSELF!

COVER UP!

HERE'S YOUR CHANCE TO CREATE THE FRONT COVER OF A MAGAZINE ALL OF YOUR OWN!

YOU WILL NEED: Safety scissors, glue, felt tip pens, old magazines, sequins, paint.

Draw a rectangle onto thin white card or thick white paper. Make up a fun title for your mag!

MAKE EVERYTHING REALLY BRIGHT WITH FELT TIP PENS OR PAINT.

Stick on sequins or shiny shapes for some added sparkle.

Stick on pictures of your favourite celebrities.

USE PHOTOS OF FAMILY, FRIENDS AND PETS.

You can even stick a picture of me on the front!

Issue Nº 1

Kid Stuff

MY MUSIC!

FOOTIE FUN!

ART ATTACK

JAM PACKED WITH OVER 150 PROJECTS!!!

9 771366 731011

09>

FREE ART KIT!

HOW ABOUT CREATING MAGAZINE COVERS FOR DIFFERENT PEOPLE AND DIFFERENT AGES? THINK OF DIFFERENT HOBBIES, SPORTS, PETS OR TRAVEL MAGAZINES - USE YOUR IMAGINATION!

YOU COULD GO ON TO CREATE THE REST OF THE MAGAZINE TOO! WRITE ARTICLES, DRAW PICTURES, CREATE PUZZLES AND MAKE UP INTERVIEWS!

SWAP SKIN!

WHY NOT PLAY AROUND WITH ANIMAL SKIN DESIGNS? IT'S A BIT FREAKY, BUT LOTS OF FUN!

YOU WILL NEED:
Paper, coloured pens.

1 Draw a simple outline of an animal such as an elephant like this.

2 Think of the most unlikely skin that it might have – this elephant's going to have a ladybird's coat, for example!

3 Colour him in – and he becomes a sort of 'elebird'!

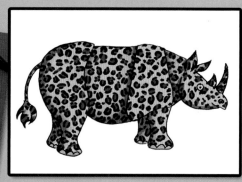

I'm giving this rhinoceros a leopard skin.

It's a 'leoponosceros'!

This giraffe's got zebra skin!

It's a 'gebra'!

Have fun making up names for your animals – this spiky dog's wearing a hedgehog's coat – it's a hedgedog! Or, what about this alligator with rat skin – it's a ratigator!

TRY IT YOURSELF!

PENGUIN PALS!

USE THE NATURAL SHAPE OF A COUPLE OF BALLOONS TO CREATE THESE CUTE LITTLE PENGUIN BUDDIES!

1 Blow up two balloons into two different sizes, one small and one a bit bigger. Balance them in bowls and cover them with six layers of papier maché to create hard shells.

2 Pop the balloons when they are completely dry. Cut out cardboard feet and tape them to the bottom of each shell.

3 Add three more papier maché layers to the feet and over the holes at the top. Leave them to dry again.

PVA

When they're dry, paint your penguins white all over. Then paint their feet orange and their bodies black with white tummies. Add a fish and face details.

3D CARDS!

SAY IT WITH FLOWERS!

YOU WILL NEED: Coloured card, tissue paper, pipe cleaners, a cocktail stick, coloured paper, glue, safety scissors, ribbon, googly eyes, craft foam, paint.

1 Make a bunch of flowers by cutting petal shapes from card, or tissue paper, and taping them to a pipe cleaner for a stalk.

2 Make a paper cone and secure it in place. Glue the flowers inside the cone.

3 Stick the cone to the front of a piece of folded, coloured card.

4 Finally, add a ribbon bow and write a message on the front of your card. How about using 3D paint?

Thanks a Bunch!

44

BAD HAIR DAY?

HAIR TODAY!

1 Fold a piece of coloured card in half to make the card. Stick cut-out shapes on the front to form a body. You'll need a t-shirt, some arms and a head shape. I've added a brush as well.

2 Add details to the face and stick on a pair of googly eyes.

3 Make small holes all the way around the head. Twist some pipe cleaners around a cocktail stick and push one through each hole, securing them in place on the other side with sticky tape.

4 Finally, write a message at the top of your card.

BUG OUT!

1 To create this 3D bug, stick some pipe cleaner legs onto the front of a piece of folded card.

2 From craft foam (or thick card), cut out an oval-shaped body and stick it onto the legs. I used sticky tabs to make it look 3-dimensional.

3 Stick on a head and decorate the body with other pieces of foam. Add googly eyes and some pipe cleaner antennae.

4 Finally, add a message to the front of your card.

Be my LOVE BUG

45

WINDOW BOX!

BRIGHTEN UP YOUR BEDROOM OR MAKE IT AS A GIFT!

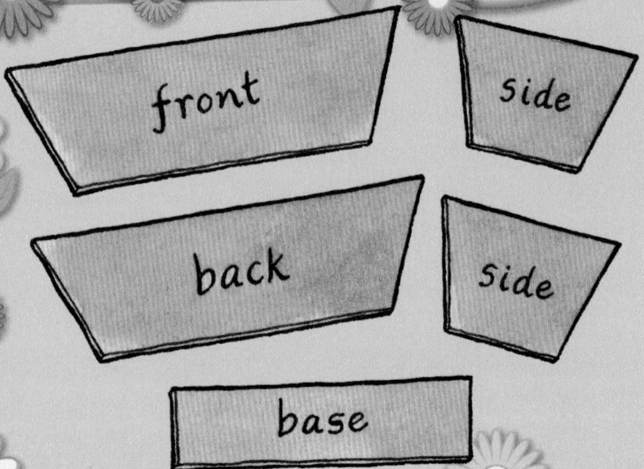

front   side

back   side

base

1 Cut out the five pieces you need to make the box using this picture as a guide for the shapes. You can make the box any size you like. You'll need two sides, a front and back and a base.

2 Stick the box together using sticky tape. Mix PVA glue with water and soak kitchen roll in the mixture to make a pulp. Use this to create a pattern on the outside of your box. Leave it to dry thoroughly.

PVA

3 Cover the whole thing with two layers of papier maché and leave it to dry before painting it any colour you like.

4 Fill the box with polystyrene, or place modelling clay in the bottom. This is to stick the flowers in. You can then use brown tissue paper or kitchen roll painted brown for soil. Check out the next page to see how to make some flowers.

LARGE PINK DAISY

Cut out a big flower shape and two small circles from thick card. Stick the circles together in the centre of the flower, cover them with papier maché, then paint them. Wrap string around a stick and paint it green to make the stalk. Attach it to the flower using glue. Make leaves from the lid of an egg box painted green.

TULIPS

Cut up the bottom of an egg box. Paint it inside and out and make a hole in the centre. Push a straw through the hole and snip the end to make stamens. Paint the straw green.

BLUEBELLS

Make the stalks in the same way as the ivy stems, but instead of winding the string into curly shapes, leave most of it straight but bend a section at the top. For the flowers, cut a thin strip of card with one scalloped edge. Snip along the opposite edge then fold the card round to make a bell shape. Fasten with sticky tape, paint, then thread it onto the stalk.

DAFFODILS

Cut out a flower shape with pointed petals for the outer section. For the middle section, cut the bottom half of an egg box into six sections then cut a zig-zag pattern around the top of each one. Stick the two pieces together, cover with papier maché, then paint it. Use a wooden stick or green straw for the stem. Make the leaves from pieces of thin card painted green.

SMALL PINK FLOWERS

Cut out a circle of thin card and draw a smaller circle in the centre. Snip around the edge to make thin petals. Paint, then tape or glue the flower onto a green straw.

SMALL DAISIES

Use the bottom of an egg box cut into individual sections. Snip around the edge to make the petals, then paint it. Stick it onto a green straw with PVA.

IVY/TRAILING FLOWERS

Cover a piece of string with papier maché. While it's still wet, curl it round to make it look like a vine. Leave it to dry then paint it brown. Make ivy leaves from cardboard shapes covered in papier maché and painted. The flowers can be made in the same way as the small daisies. Glue the leaves or flowers onto the vine with PVA.

SUPER SK8-BOARDS!

DESIGN YOUR DREAM BOARD! YOU CAN COPY THESE ONES OR GO WILD WITH YOUR OWN IDEAS!

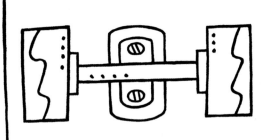

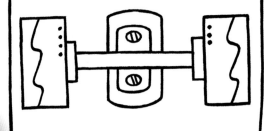

1 Trace or photocopy the skateboard template onto white paper, stick it onto card and then cut it out.

2 Decorate both sides with paints or felt tip pens.

3 Cover your skateboard with sticky-backed plastic for a durable finish!

LOOKING GOOD!

THIS BEAUTIFUL FRAME AND JEWELLERY BOX ARE FIT FOR A PRINCESS... OR A BEAUTY QUEEN!

MIRROR

1 Measure the size of the mirror you want to use then draw a frame shape onto a piece of card and cut it out. Cover it in two layers of papier maché and leave it to dry.

2 Draw some hearts, diamonds, stars, flowers and bottles/jars onto a piece of cardboard. Cut them out, cover in two layers of papier maché and leave them to dry.

3 Cover the diamonds with tin foil, then stick these and the other shapes to the frame. Paint it as shown or choose your own colours.

4 Once the paint is dry, decorate your frame with glitter glue, pom-poms and sequins. Stick pieces of foil to the front of the bottles to look like labels.

ELLERY

1 Cover an empty tea bag box with a layer of papier maché.

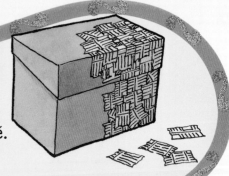

ASK AN ADULT TO HELP YOU STICK YOUR FINISHED FRAME IN PLACE!

Beauty Queen

Lotion

ART ATTACK

2

Make papier maché shapes as before and glue them in place, then paint the box and decorate it to match the frame.

HOW TO DRAW...

CHECK OUT THESE CRAZY CHARACTERS – THEN DRAW SOME OF YOUR OWN!

54

IT'S A-MAZE-ING!

HELP NEIL PICK UP ALL HIS PAINTS AND PAINTBRUSHES,
THEN FIND HIS WAY TO THE CENTRE OF THE MAZE!

START

PERFECT GARDEN!

HERE'S A CHEAP AND EASY WAY TO MAKE YOUR OWN PERFECT GARDEN!

YOU WILL NEED:

Tray, modelling clay, paper, pen, safety scissors, sponges, pencil, mirror tile, cocktail stick, drinking straw, sand, PVA glue, elastic band, bird seed, old chess piece, soil, lolly sticks, scouring pads, small artificial flowers.

1 Plan the layout of your garden on a piece of paper, so that you can check it will fit into the tray. You can do any type of garden you like – this plan has a pond, a patio, a path, a lawn and even a washing line!

2 Position the mirror tile in one corner to make a pond. To create the lawn, roll out some green soft modelling clay onto a board. It needs to be about 0.5cm thick. Use a plastic knife to create whatever shaped lawns you like then lay them carefully in position on the tray.

3 To give the modelling clay a more realistic texture, use a plastic knife, a fork or a cocktail stick to create tufts of grass.

4 To make a potted palm: cut out some leaf shapes from old green scouring pads. When you have cut enough leaf shapes, hold them together with glue, a bag tie or an elastic band. When you've made a few bundles, tie the whole lot together with wire.

5 To make a tall leylandii tree, all you need are some torn-up bits of sponge and an old pencil. Use strong glue to stick the bits of sponge onto the pencil, building up layers until you have the shape of a tree.

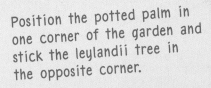

6 Position the potted palm in one corner of the garden and stick the leylandii tree in the opposite corner.

7 To make a rose flower bed, tape some cut-down drinking straws together to make a surround and fill it with soil. Pop in some small artificial flowers or cake decorations. For the path, pour in bird seed. It looks just like gravel.

8 To turn the pond into a fancy fountain, all you need is an old toy or figure. An old chess piece is perfect! Coat it in PVA glue, roll it in some fine sand, to give it a stone look, shake off the excess and allow it to dry. Place it in the middle of the mirror tile.

9 Add a washing line made from string and make some clothes out of paper. To finish, paint the leylandii bright green and the cut-down drinking straws brown to look like wood. To make a patio, you need some light coloured modelling clay. As before, just use a cocktail stick to etch a tile pattern into it. Make a deck chair from lolly sticks.

IF YOUR IDEAL GARDEN IS A SNOW-COVERED WINTER SCENE, JUST USE WHITE MODELLING CLAY, COTTON WOOL AND GLITTER TO GIVE IT A COOL FROSTED EFFECT!

TRY IT YOURSELF!

ANCIENT SCROLL!

WRITE A UNIQUE LETTER OR CREATE A SCROLL FOR A SCHOOL PLAY...

YOU WILL NEED:

Sheet of cartridge paper, brown watercolour paint or old teabag, pen and ink, brown crayon or pencil, piece of ribbon, string.

1 Start with a sheet of cartridge paper. To make it look old, like parchment, either paint it with a watery wash of brown watercolour paint or dab it all over with a soggy teabag. Leave it to dry.

2 Write your wording, in old-fashioned hand writing, using a pen with brown or black ink. You could write a letter or a proclamation.

3 When the ink has dried, fold and re-fold the paper several times to make it look weathered and old.

4 Tear a thin strip off all the edges, for a ragged effect. Then rub all the torn edges with a brown crayon or pencil.

GLUE TWO PIECES OF RIBBON IN PLACE AT THE TOP, THEN ADD A BIG BLOB OF RED ACRYLIC PAINT.

COPY OLD-FASHIONED WRITING FROM BOOKS OR THE INTERNET.

DIP A PAINTBRUSH IN WATER AND DRAG THE BRISTLE OVER THE TIP OF A BROWN WATERCOLOUR CRAYON, FLICKING THE COLOUR ON TO THE PAPER.

FINALLY ROLL YOUR ANCIENT SCROLL UP AND TIE IT WITH A PIECE OF STRING OR RIBBON.